Also by Bob Hartman:
The Precious Pearl
The Busy Builders
One Sheep Short
Bob Hartman's Rhyming Bible
The Link-it-Up Bible
The Tell-it-Together Gospel

The Lion Storyteller Bible 25th Anniversary Edition
Welcome to the Journey
Where Do I Come from?

————————

The original version of this story is found in the Gospel of Luke, where Jesus tells a parable:

'A man prepared a great feast and sent out many invitations. When the banquet was ready, he sent his servant to tell the guests, 'Come, the banquet is ready.' But they all began making excuses. One said, 'I have just bought a field and must inspect it. Please excuse me.' Another said, 'I have just bought five pairs of oxen, and I want to try them out. Please excuse me.' Another said, 'I just got married, so I can't come.'

'The servant returned and told his master what they had said. His master was furious and said, 'Go quickly into the streets and alleys of the town and invite the poor, the crippled, the blind, and the lame.' After the servant had done this, he reported, 'There is still room for more.' So his master said, 'Go out into the country lanes and behind the hedges and urge anyone you find to come, so that the house will be full. For none of those I first invited will get even the smallest taste of my banquet.'

Luke 14: 15–24 (New Living Translation)

————————

First published in Great Britain in 2022

Society for Promoting Christian Knowledge
36 Causton Street, London SW1P 4ST
www.spck.org.uk

Text copyright © Bob Hartman 2022
Illustrations copyright © Mark Beech 2022

British Library Cataloguing-in-Publication Data
A catalogue record for this book is avaliable from the British Library

ISBN 978–0–281–08540–8

Printed by Imago

Produced on paper from sustainable forests

Bob Hartman

THE FANTASTIC FEAST

Fantastic illustrations by

Mark Beech

'A banquet!' said the master.
'I want to host a feast!'
He posted invitations to the
west and to the east.

4

And when the pots were flowing with the broth of boiled beast,
he sent out his best servant with this message to release:

The jellies are w^obbling, **blobby** and *unsteady*,

the pies are full of pie stuff, big as your head-y,

6

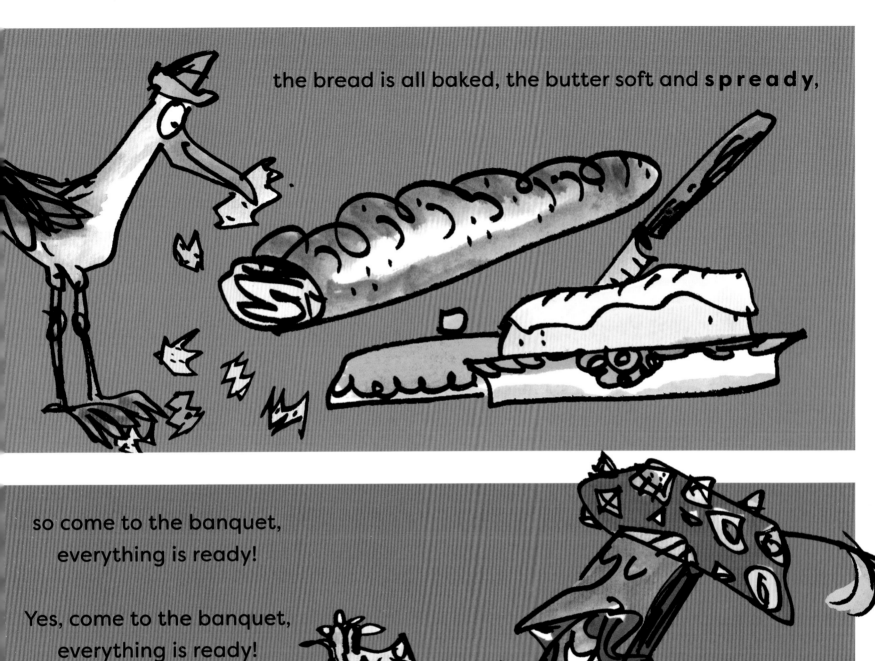

the bread is all baked, the butter soft and **s p r e a d y**,

so come to the banquet,
   everything is ready!

Yes, come to the banquet,
   everything is ready!

But when the answers all came back, much to his surprise,
the servant was amazed at all the reasons they devised.

The guests made their excuses, they all apologized,
and no one seemed to rate the master's jellies or his pies.

9

'I'm sorry,' said a man with a brand spanking new field.
'I have to check my land to see what it will yield.

I'd love to wrap my lips around your great big slap-up meal,
but I'm gonna have to miss it, and that's just how I feel.'

'I'm sorry,' said a man, who'd bought five yokes of ox.
'They just arrived today (in quite a massive box!)

I have to see if they're healthy, check them for the pox.
I have no time for banquets or after-dinner talks!'

'I'm sorry,' said another. 'I have a brand-new bride.
The wedding was emotional, no eye was left uncried.

14

And so I cannot leave her, our knot is truly tied.
I'll offer my apology and stay here by her side.'

The servant told the master what everyone had said.

The master was not happy, and his face turned angry red.

'Go out into the streets, to where
the poor all lay their heads.
Extend my invitation to all
those folk instead!'

So out into alleys and city
streets he went.

'A meal has been prepared,
a fortune has been spent!

18

The blind and lame are welcome
and those without a cent.

Don't hesitate and don't be late
for this great big event!'

The jellies are w^obbling,
blobby and *unsteady*,

the pies are full of pie stuff,
big as your head-y,

20

the bread is all baked,
the butter soft and **spready**,

so come to the banquet,
everything is ready!
Yes, come to the banquet,
everything is ready!

Then, at the invitation, a crowd of people came.
And there were no excuses from the poor and blind and lame.

Everyone was welcomed,
everyone the same.
'Can't wait to feast on boiled beast!'
these brand new guests exclaimed.

'Everyone is seated, but there's still room for more,'

the servant told the master, who opened up the door.

'Go out into the fields,' he said,
'the highways and the shore.'

'I want to fill my house,' he cried.
'Invite! Insist! Implore!'

25

The jellies are w^obbling,
blobby and *unsteady*,

the pies are full of pie stuff,
big as your head-y,

the bread is all baked,
the butter soft and **s p r e a d y**,

so come to the banquet,
everything is ready!
Yes, come to the banquet,
everything is ready!

27

Now the place was crowded, with two on every chair,

hanging from the chandeliers, sitting on the stairs.

Perched upon the windowsills, they didn't have a care,
city folk and country folk. Folk from everywhere!

When the house was filled up with the lowly and the least,

the master wined and dined his friends,
the party never ceased.

Then someone shouted out aloud, mouth filled with boiled beast,
'Blessed is the one who eats in God's forever feast!'